D1090868

Dena, Anael   25147

Numbers

MR 16'98
 JE 17'98
  AG 12'98
   SE 2'98
DE 7'99

SE 6'00

OC 22'02

DEMCO

Amer. Lib. Preview 15.00 2-11-88 50

LITTLE MOUSE'S LEARN-AND-PLAY

Numbers

1

2

5

8

9

3

4

6

7

10

For a free color catalog describing Gareth Stevens' list of high-quality books and multimedia programs, call 1-800-542-2595 (USA) or 1-800-461-9120 (Canada). Gareth Stevens Publishing's Fax: (414) 225-0377.
See our catalog, too, on the World Wide Web: http://gsinc.com

Library of Congress Cataloging-in-Publication Data

Dena, Anaël.
    [Chiffres. English]
    Numbers / text by Anaël Dena ; illustrated by Christel Desmoinaux.
       p. cm. — (Little Mouse's learn-and-play)
      Summary: Artwork and simple text present a variety of activities
through which the reader can learn about numbers.
     ISBN 0-8368-1986-1 (lib. bdg)
     1. Mathematics—Juvenile literature. [1. Mathematics.]
  I. Desmoinaux, Christel, ill. II. Title. III. Series: Dena, Anaël.
Little Mouse's learn-and-play.
QA40.5.D4513   1997
513.2—dc21   97-20904

This North American edition first published in 1997 by
Gareth Stevens Publishing
1555 North RiverCenter Drive, Suite 201
Milwaukee, Wisconsin 53212 USA

This U.S. edition © 1997 by Gareth Stevens, Inc. Original © 1995 by Editions Nathan, Paris, France. Titre de l'edition originale (original title): *Les Chiffres* publiée par Les Editions Nathan, Paris. Additional end matter © 1997 by Gareth Stevens, Inc.

Translated from the French by Janet Neis.
U.S. editors: Patricia Lantier-Sampon and Rita Reitci
Editorial assistant: Diane Laska

Printed in the United States of America

1 2 3 4 5 6 7 8 9 01 00 99 98 97

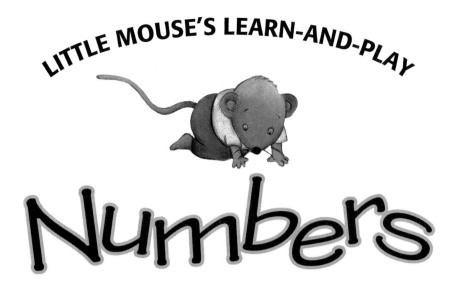

LITTLE MOUSE'S LEARN-AND-PLAY

Numbers

by Anaël Dena
Illustrations by Christel Desmoinaux

Gareth Stevens Publishing
MILWAUKEE

ONE little rabbit visits a field and picks a pretty flower. A sheep thinks the flower looks tasty, but continues to graze on the sweet green grass.

Can you find **ONE** of anything on this page?

In Grandfather's attic,
TWO rabbits open an old
chest. Look what they find
inside — two dusty books,
two old shoes, and two hats
for playing dress-up!

Can you find anything
else in groups of **TWO**?

THREE rabbits enjoy
going to the park.
They play on slides and
bouncy rides. They run
around, playing tag.
What fun they have!

Can you find anything in groups of **THREE**?

What a beautiful snowman
the **FOUR** rabbits have made!
He has a carrot for a nose, a cap
to warm his snowy head, and
pebbles to button his wintry coat.

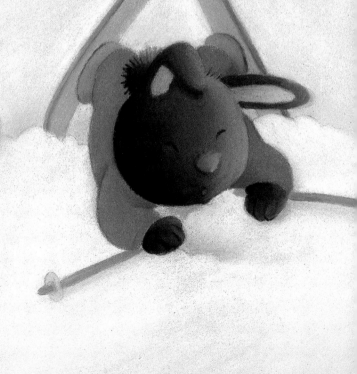

Can you find anything
in groups of **FOUR**?

FIVE rabbits attend a birthday party. Everyone brings a present and eats lots of good food.

Can you find anything
in groups of **FIVE**?

SIX rabbits have
packed their suitcases
and backpacks for
a trip. Goodbye!
See you soon!

Can you find anything
in groups of **SIX**?

SEVEN rabbits
play at the beach.
They gather seashells,
make sand castles,
and go swimming.
What fun in the sun!

Can you find anything
in groups of **SEVEN**?

EIGHT rascally rabbits make funny faces in school. Look out, rabbits — here comes the teacher!

Can you find anything in groups of **EIGHT**?

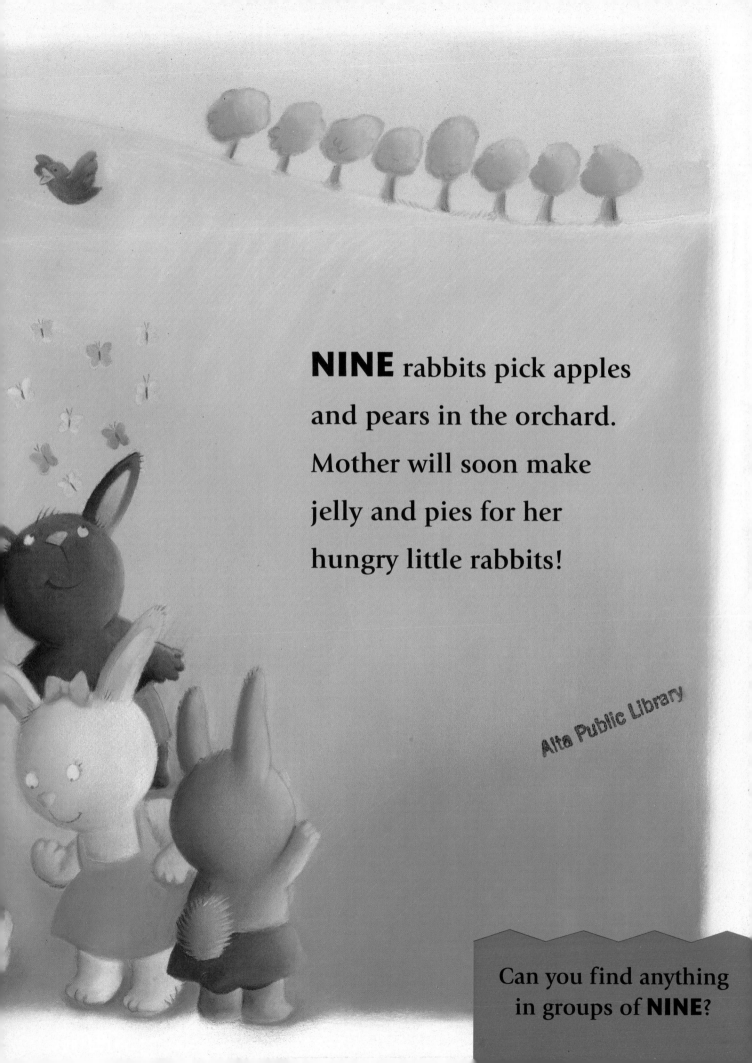

NINE rabbits pick apples and pears in the orchard. Mother will soon make jelly and pies for her hungry little rabbits!

Can you find anything in groups of **NINE**?

Fish and frogs jump
and play in the pond.
When it gets late, **TEN**
rabbits say goodnight
to the ducklings.

Can you find anything
in groups of **TEN**?

Match the rabbits

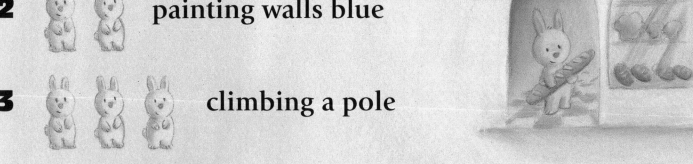

1   buying bread

2   painting walls blue

3   climbing a pole

4   wearing their neckties

5   taking a bubbly bath

6   doing their exercises

7   playing their trumpets

8   running a race

9   looking at a big chocolate egg

10   sleeping in their bed

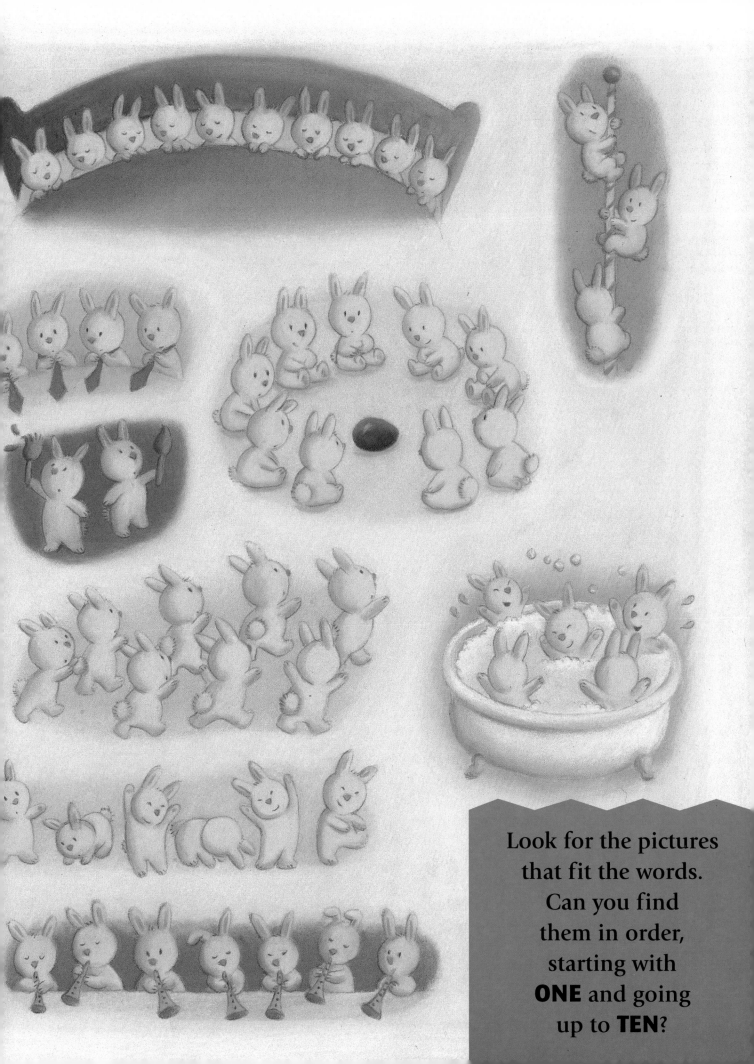

Look for the pictures
that fit the words.
Can you find
them in order,
starting with
ONE and going
up to **TEN**?

Can you match the socks?

This little rabbit has trouble
keeping his clothes neat.
He put his shoes away,
two by two, but his socks
are all mixed up!

Help the little
rabbit match
up his pairs
of socks.

Big brother, little brother

Little rabbit and his big brother
are going to ride their bikes.
They decide to take a few extra
supplies along, just in case.

Which rabbit is shorter? Which rabbit is taller? Can you tell which things belong to each rabbit?

Rabbit cousins

Rabbit cousins line
up from short to tall.
Rudy Rabbit is a giant.
He is so big he doesn't
fit on the page!

Where is
Rudy Rabbit?
Which cousin
is the shortest?
Who wears the
smallest bow tie?
Who wears
the largest?

Rabbits playing

The rabbits are playing on the floor with their favorite toys.

Who has more cars?
Who has fewer rings?
Who has more
stones? Who has
fewer marbles? Who
has more sticks?

The picnic

The rabbits decide to have
a picnic in the meadow.
They bring a basket
filled with lots of
good things to eat.

Are there as many
ewes as lambs?
Do the rabbits have
the same number
of sandwiches?
Are there as many
plates as rabbits?
Are there as many
apples as rabbits?

The tortoise race

The rabbits cheer at the annual tortoise race. The tortoises race slowly to the finish line.

How many tortoises
are on the red team?
How many on
the yellow team?
How many tortoises
are there in all?
Which tortoise
finishes first?
How many
cabbages will they
get as prizes?

The collectors

Each rabbit brother
has a picture collection.
One collects fish, and the
other collects butterflies.

How many
butterfly pictures
are on the wall?
How many
fish pictures?
How many
pictures does
each rabbit have
on the floor?
How many
yellow butterflies
are there in all?

The rabbit race game

To play, you need one token for each player and a single die. Each player places his or her token on a START space. The players take turns rolling the die and moving the token the number of spaces shown on the die. The player who gets to the FINISH line first wins.

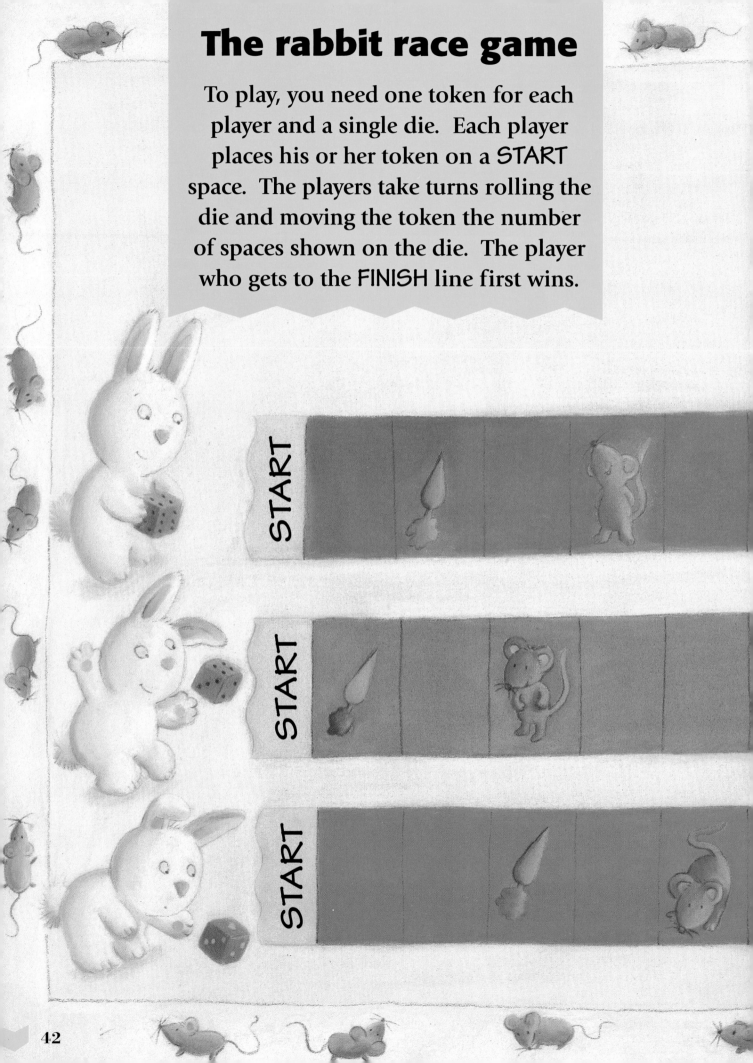

START

START

START

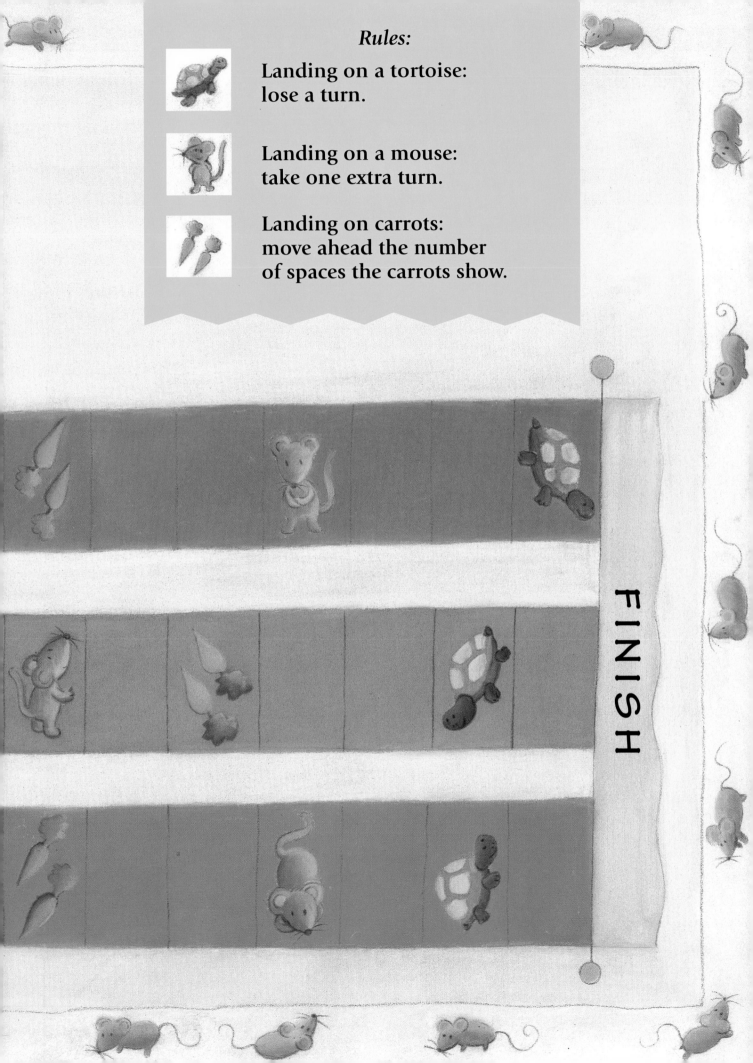

Rules:

Landing on a tortoise: lose a turn.

Landing on a mouse: take one extra turn.

Landing on carrots: move ahead the number of spaces the carrots show.

FINISH

One hundred rabbits to count!

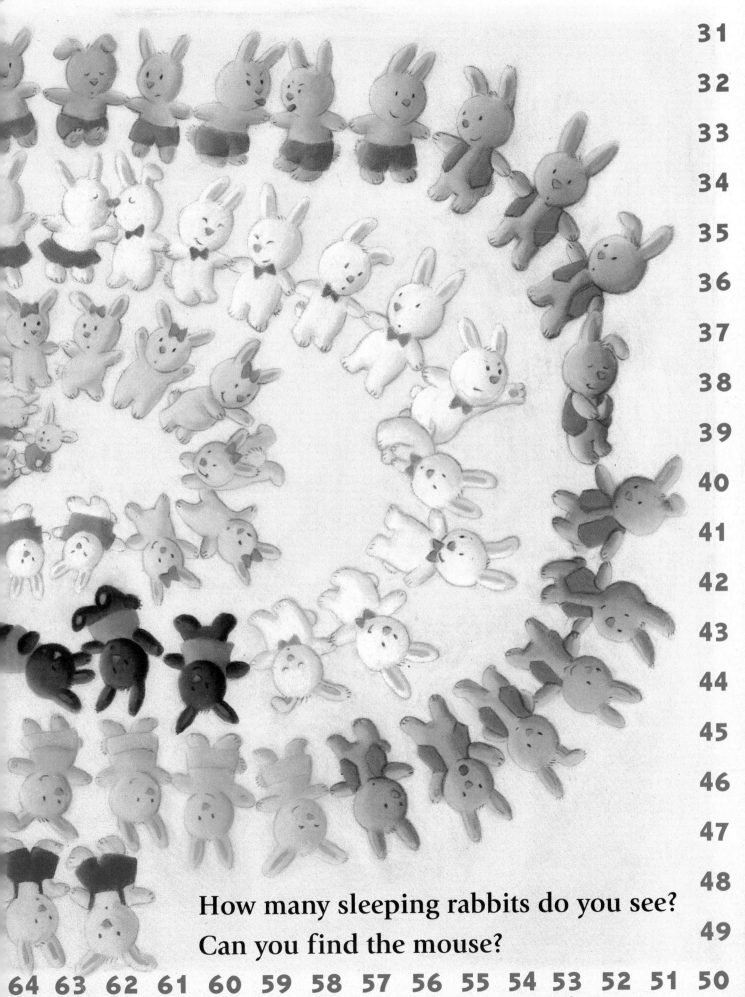

13 14 15 16 17 18 19 20 21 22 23 24 25 26 27 28 29 30

31

32

33

34

35

36

37

38

39

40

41

42

43

44

45

46

47

48

How many sleeping rabbits do you see?

49

Can you find the mouse?

64 63 62 61 60 59 58 57 56 55 54 53 52 51 50

Books

Blast Off! A Space Counting Book.
Norma Cole (Charlesbridge
Publishing)

Counting. Brenda Walpole
(Gareth Stevens)

Counting on Frank. Rod Clement
(Gareth Stevens)

First Step Math series. Rose Griffiths
(Gareth Stevens)

*Five Little Monsters Jumping on the
Bed.* Tedd Arnold (Scholastic)

*Gathering: A Northwoods Counting
Book.* Betsy Bowen (Little, Brown)

*Hold the Bus! A Counting Book
from 1 to 10.* Arlene Alda
(Troll Communications)

Let's Count, Dracula. Alan Benjamin
(Simon and Schuster Children's)

My First Numbers. Francoise Audry-
Iljie and Thierry Courtin (Barron)

Numbers. Science Works! series.
Steve Parker (Gareth Stevens)

Odds and Evens: A Number Book.
Heidi Goennel (Morrow)

The Science Book of Numbers.
J. Challoner (Harcourt Brace)

Ten Little Bunnies. Lisa Bassett
(Random House Value)

Two Crows Counting. Doris Orgel
(Gareth Stevens)

Zoe's Sheep. Rose Bursik (H. Holt)

Videos

Adventures in Woollyville.
(Library Video)

Best Counting Video Ever.
(Music for Little People, Inc.)

Clifford's Fun with Numbers.
(Kimbo Educational)

Counting by Tens and Fives.
(Phoenix/BFA Films and Video)

Hello Numbers. (Good Apple)

Web Sites

www.worldvillage.com/kidz/
bilybear/mapedit/math1.htm

www.worldvillage.com/kidz/
bilybear/puzzles/dot2dot.htm

Glossary – Index

annual: happening once a year (*p. 38*).

attend: to be present at; to visit; to go to (*p. 14*).

attic: a room or space just below the roof of a building (*p. 9*).

backpack: a sack made of heavy material worn on the back to carry things (*p. 17*).

chest: a box with a lid used to keep belongings (*p. 9*).

collection: a group of objects gathered for study or show (*p. 40*).

cousin: a child of one's uncle or aunt (*pp. 32, 33*).

die: a small cube marked on each side with dots from one to six, usually used in twos, called a pair of dice (*p. 42*).

ewe: a female sheep (*p. 37*).

favorite: something that is liked more than the others (*p. 34*).

graze: to feed on grass (*p. 7*).

match: to find two or more objects that have something alike, such as a color or a shape (*pp. 26, 28, 29*).

meadow: low-lying, level, moist grassland (*p. 36*).

neat: clean; orderly; free from dirt or mess (*p. 28*).

orchard: several fruit or nut trees planted together (*p. 23*).

pair: two of anything, such as a pair of shoes or a pair of dice (*p. 29*).

pebbles: small round stones (*p. 12*).

rascally: behaving in a mischievous way (*p. 21*).

suitcase: a flat, rectangular bag in which to pack clothes to take traveling (*p. 17*).

token: a small piece used by a player in a board game (*p. 42*).

tortoise: a turtle that lives on land (*pp. 38, 39, 43*).